Contemporary
INTERIORS

ROOM by ROOM

GLOUCESTER MASSACHUSETTS

ROCKPORT
PUBLISHERS

CAROL MEREDITH

First published in the United States of America by
Rockport Publishers, Inc.
33 Commercial Street
Gloucester, Massachusetts 01930-5089
Telephone: (978) 282-9590
Facsimile: (978) 283-2742

Distributed to the book trade and art trade in the United States by
North Light Books, an imprint of
F & W Publications
1507 Dana Avenue
Cincinnati, Ohio 45207
Telephone: (800) 289-0963

Other distribution by
Rockport Publishers, Inc.
Gloucester, Massachusetts 01930-5089

ISBN 1-56496-427-2

10 9 8 7 6 5 4 3 2 1

Cover Design: Elastic Design, Concord, Massachusetts
Book Design: Argus Visual Communication, Boston, Massachusetts
Front cover image: Warren Jagger, page 52
Back cover images: Warren Jagger, pages 19, 52, 76; and Paul Rocheleau, page 150

Printed in China

Dedication

Dedicated to my daughters Anne and Aleisha Reynolds, whose youthful perspective helps keep me focused on the here and now of contemporary living.

Acknowledgments

First and foremost, I extend my sincere appreciation to interior designer Lloy Hack, whose perceptive insights guided the text of *Room by Room: Contemporary Interiors.* During numerous long sessions, Lloy eloquently shared her knowledge of contemporary style, conveying her passion for twentieth-century design in a way that has energized and enriched my own life as well as the following pages.

Rockport Publishers Acquisitions Editor Rosalie Grattaroti, the guiding light behind the *Room by Room* series, persuaded me that I just had to write this book. Thank you, Rosalie, and thanks to the entire staff at Rockport. In particular, I am grateful to my editor, Martha Wetherill, who is an exceptional woman: supportive and encouraging, gentle yet solid, warm and professional. Thanks, too, to Jeanine Caunt, who willingly stepped in to oversee completion of the detailed editing process; Lynne Havighurst, Rockport's art director; and Madeline Perri, who copyedited the manuscript.

The architects and interior designers responsible for the remarkable rooms in this book deserve special recognition, not only for their contributions here, but also for achieving a degree of professional excellence that elevates the entire field of residential design. I also extend my thanks to the many contributing photographers, especially to Tim Street-Porter, whose superb images are featured extensively.

Finally, my deep appreciation goes to my husband, David Reynolds, who eased my journey through *Room by Room: Contemporary Interiors* by listening during the challenges, celebrating the landmarks, and sharing the day-to-day gift of his loving, grace-filled presence.

Contents

Foreword

Lloy Hack, ASID, IIDA

In the beginning of any residential project, the owners, along with their interior designer and architect, make the single most significant decision of the entire creative process. That choice is to create a home whose design responds to the present time and place, or to imagine a time out of history and then create a solution imitating the styles and preferences of that era.

After three decades of designing award-winning interiors, I believe more strongly than ever in the value of making the first choice.

More than any other style of residential design, a contemporary approach responds to the real experiences, attitudes, emotional needs, location, financial situation, and lifestyles of the people who will live in the home. Each of these elements and ideas influences the design process, directly or indirectly affecting everything from how open spaces are and how they relate to one another, to how money is allocated, to the kinds of materials used in the furniture and architectural detailing.

As you look at the marvelous range of contemporary spaces in *Room by Room: Contemporary Interiors*, look for evidence of the modern-day attitudes and ideas driving the design decisions. Very frequently those attitudes and ideas are about encouraging human interaction. Today's kitchens, for instance, frequently include stools at work surfaces and counters to encourage family members and friends to gather before mealtime. This design solution responds to current social attitudes that are very different than even two decades ago.

The rooms in this book also convey the nearly universal modern-day attitude that life at home should be physically comfortable and informal. In my interior design practice I have rarely encountered a client who chooses the opposite, even for the traditionally "formal" parts of the house. Comfort is contemporary.

Yet another rewarding aspect of contemporary design is its general rejection of pretense. Like modern-day culture that encourages people to be more genuine and open, contemporary design attempts to represent things exactly as they are. That means materials, structures, furniture styles, and relationships between interior and exterior spaces all celebrate the reality of the individual parts.

Unlike aesthetic styles that focus on uniformity, contemporary design thinking, like contemporary society, cultivates the careful inclusion of diversity. This does not, however, mean that the desired result comes without rigorous discipline. On the contrary, the very art of interior design is its discipline. Discipline focuses the thinking and decision-making process to support the central goal of creating an interior that is the clearest possible expression of the discrete design elements and the people who will live there. Art can be the result. A contemporary environment arising out of this discipline, this consciousness, has a lovely connectedness that engages and embraces not only the day-to-day residents and designers who created it, but also others who encounter it—including those who enter in through the exquisite photographs of contemporary homes featured in this book. Dive in, the water is crystal clear.

Lloy Hack, ASID, IIDA, is principal-in-charge of design of Lloy Hack Associates, a full-service interior design firm in Boston, Massachusetts. Her work has been widely recognized with awards and publication, most recently with the Fourth Annual Will Ching Design Award and an Outstanding Achievement Award presented by the International Interior Design Association. Before forming Lloy Hack Associates in 1978, Ms. Hack headed interior design departments for various architectural firms, including the legendary Marcel Breuer and Associates.

Carol Meredith *Introduction*

"Be in the present," encourage the world's great spiritual teachers. True happiness and inner peace come not with focusing on the past or the future, but with consciously living in the here and now.

Many people will attest that this philosophy enhances human existence when applied not only to our minds and hearts, but also to our homes. After all, the conviction that the environment has a profound impact on human experience is the driving force behind architecture and interior design. To live in a house that is contemporary—that is, of the current time—may indeed affect our ability to live our lives in the present.

In the years flanking the turn of the millennium, just what makes a home contemporary? That question is explored through the radiant photographs in the following chapters of *Room by Room: Contemporary Interiors*. What does it mean for residential architecture and furnishings to be of the present time, relatively unencumbered by the conventions and styles of previous centuries?

Without a doubt, contemporary style is underscored by the revolutionary thinking that fueled the Modern movement, a sharp reaction to the excessively grandiose architecture and interiors of the nineteenth century. Beginning in Europe, Modernism's radically unfettered design broke on the international scene in the 1920s.

Soon thereafter, Modernism became the symbol of the free world, with the traditions of the old world and their associated totalitarian governments replaced by a clean, modest approach. New technology and materials developed for industrial uses, rather than being ignored in residential design, were embraced and used to create innovative environments intended to complement life in the machine age. In the words of Le Corbusier, one of the twentieth century's most influential architects, the ideal house was a "machine for living": functional, rational, beautiful in its simplicity, and free of ornament merely for ornament's sake.

In many ways, the Modernists' enormous influence continues today. Contemporary architecture and furniture design, while not as narrowly defined as pure Modernism, share the Modernist ideal of engaging the present reality of the world. Screening reality—making things appear different from what they are—is eschewed.

Rather than using a material in spite of itself, overcoming its inherent qualities in order to conform with current style, today's designers celebrate the intrinsic nature of materials. Instead of masking a house's steel posts and beams, contemporary architecture incorporates them as is into the overall design. The same approach carries through to furniture. A glass surface on a table may be slightly raised from the supporting structure so the glass's unique qualities can be seen and appreciated. In contemporary design, this sort of well-articulated expression is valued for its honesty and elegance.

Another characteristic of contemporary residences is extensive glazing (windows and glass doors and walls) that dissolves the boundary between interior and exterior. To support the ideal of space flowing uninterrupted between inside and out, windows often lack a head or frame and instead are set directly into grooves in the ceiling or floor. Relationships between interior spaces are treated with care, too, which is especially relevant since so many contemporary houses have open plans. Indeed, openness and light—virtues lifted up by early Modernists—are highly valued today.

While owing much to the early decades of Modernism, contemporary interiors are unique. Aesthetic rigidity is a thing of the past, as are strict rules governing design decisions. Instead of paying homage to dogmatic principles of an intellectual movement, people today are more concerned with expressing personal identity through the home. Professional interior designers and architects continue to be important players in the creation of noteworthy residences, but their clients exude a new confidence, an assurance that they can decide on their own what they like and don't like. As a result, today's homes tend to be highly individualistic and often idiosyncratic.

This growing fascination with developing one's own personal style has led to interiors characterized by eclecticism, the bringing together of all kinds of twentieth-century designs. Nowadays, mixing first- and second-tier pieces is altogether acceptable, such as pairing George Nelson's esteemed Coconut chair with a funky but beloved 1950s-era lamp found in a junk shop. Putting together items from various decades is perfectly fine, too, as in placing a new Italian-designed sofa next to Marcel Breuer's groundbreaking 1928 tubular-steel cantilevered chair. In numerous instances, contemporary design is purposely irreverent, delighting in odd juxtapositions that introduce a touch of wit and whimsy.

While contemporary design typically reduces clutter in order to provide a free forum for enjoying space, line, form, light, color, and texture, most homeowners aren't interested in committing to the discipline required for a truly minimalist interior. A more important value today is physical comfort. This priority is particularly evident in furniture design, with seating characterized by deep, ample cushions that provide gentle support for stretching out with a book or settling in for a long, intimate conversation.

This is an exciting time in the history of architecture and interior design. More than ever before, the focus is on everyday people, with home environments fostering open attitudes, relaxation, a spirit of fun, and interpersonal connections—all high priorities in current culture. Contemporary design, with its responsiveness to the human dimension and today's lifestyles, holds the promise of helping people live in the present—in easygoing environments where it's a pleasure to simply *be*.

Contemporary Entrances

As you begin to plan your entryway, think about the ideas and feelings about your home that you want to convey through the design.

Entrances have a profound psychological impact on those who come and go because they create a first impression and also convey symbolic meaning. Some contemporary doors, for instance, are heavy, wooden barriers offering the reassurance of protection from the world, while others are framed transparent or translucent glass that invites the outside in.

Most entryways accommodate very few pieces of furniture; make sure the items you select immediately establish the contemporary aesthetic that will unfold throughout the rest of the house. A single distinctive chair—whether a taut, linear form made of inexpensive materials, or a Modern classic such as Mies van der Rohe's Barcelona chair—can go a long way toward setting a style. Avoid clutter in favor of a clean look, choosing only a few focal points such as an exotic, cutting-edge mirror or avant-garde painting, a sleek table or hand-crafted console. Tables and chairs have their practical side, as well, providing surfaces to hold items in transit and places to sit while pulling on boots and coats for inclement weather.

When designing large entrances, long hallways, and other transition areas, recall the experience of driving an automobile down a highway. In a car, the sense of movement comes from the rhythmic passing of regularly spaced utility poles and other markers on the road. Similarly, movement through circulation areas becomes noteworthy when the space is articulated, that is, divided into distinct parts by a progression of artwork or a series of architectural features such as pilasters or niches. Lighting also plays a key role in articulating transition spaces.

Stairways, typically celebrated in grand traditional residences, are particularly exciting elements in contemporary homes. Here, the Modern idea of reducing a functional element to its simplest form often is carried to an extreme, with nothing more than stair treads and stringers suspended in space like airborne sculpture. Balusters and balustrades run the gamut from purely functional forms, to designs that are highly expressive of construction materials, to witty renditions of contemporary style.

In a departure from the Modernist philosophy that urges the exposure of even the most basic components of functional design elements, this contemporary entry hall conjures a sense of mystery. A dreamlike surface covered with an abstract design creates the illusion of a painted wall, but closer inspection reveals the doorknobs and panels of folding closet doors. Design: Mary Knackstedt; Photo: Bill Rothschild

The sturdy horizontal planks and hefty frame of the front door express the idea of a protective barrier, while the transparency of the glass sidelights serves as a counterpoint. The absence of artwork and furnishings keeps the focus on the door's basic function. In another part of the house (left), the sense of movement through a long corridor is emphasized by floorboards laid in the same direction as the flow of traffic and stately pylons marking progression through the space. Design: Dan Phipps and Associates; Photo: John Sutton

Furnishings and details can establish contemporary style in any house, even older residences with classical bones. Note how new baseboards strike a perfect balance between Modernism and the more traditional design of the crown moldings. Design: Stedila Design; Photo: Richard Mandelkorn

Long entrances and hallways benefit from careful articulation that emphasizes movement. By using the design device of sequential framed openings, this transition area gives the illusion of passing through a larger space. Design: Rick Garofalo. Repertoire; Photo: Eric Roth

This entry's powerful sightline to the fireplace immediately draws people to the heart of the house. The resulting psychological impact is considerable: the entry and fireplace say "welcome" and "home. The design of the door is strongly asymmetrical, a common approach in contemporary design. Design: Dan Phipps and Associates; Photo: John Sutton

In contrast to entrances that immediately reveal intimate spaces, this one—in the spirit of Frank Lloyd Wright's philosophy on entries–offers only glimpses. This entry hall is particularly coy in that the use of stucco, a material typically used on exterior walls, makes the space seem like it is outside as much as inside. Interior Design: Lloy Hack Associates; Architecture: Based on a design by William P. Bruder; Photo: Warren Jagger

This atrium entrance is bathed in natural light, while louvers outdoors provide privacy from the street. A dramatic semicircular form accommodates a stairway descending from the entry hall. Many descending staircases look like dark holes in the floor, but this stair is an exciting architectural event. Design: Shubin + Donaldson Architects; Photos: Farshid Assassi

Lighting, cabinetry, and windows visually break up hallways while meeting practical needs. When halls and stairs open to one another, as in this soaring two-story transition area, harmony is created by consistently carrying through materials and forms. Design: Peter L. Gluck and Partners, Architects; Photo: Paul Warchol

Today's interiors incorporate witty juxtapositions, as in this eccentric pairing of an ornate cast-iron stair rail and International-style architectural forms. Art and artifacts are showcased in lighted display niches that draw attention, while a warm color scheme also invites people into the space. Design: Currimbhoy Design; Photo: Peter Paige

This entrance speaks the language of a reinforced castle; its studded wooden door presents clearly an apparently impermeable barrier to the world. The curved stair and small punched windows build on the castle vocabulary. Design: Piers Gough, CZWG Architects; Photo: Tim Street-Porter

In a Texas residence, Modernism meets the vernacular, with the sleek chairs, avant-garde floor lamp, and plain black balusters—the essence of simplicity—happily coexisting with the textural rusticity of native stone walls. Smooth, cool floor tiles help bridge the two worlds. Design: Tonny Foy; Photo: Peter Paige

In a powerful play of line in space, the angles of
the split-run stairway are juxtaposed against the
orthogonal geometry of the yellow columns and
beam. The columns provide continuity and rhythm
as they repeat through the circulation area. Design:
Stuart Disston, Austin Patterson Disston Architects;
Photos: John Kane

This lively and poetic design is a prime example
of stairway as sculpture in a contemporary residence. Twigs interwoven in the balustrade are a
delightful organic detail, visually tying the stair
to the forest outside. Design: Jill Benedict and
Peter Stempel; Photo: Eric Roth

This transition area is an excellent example of how a long space can be transformed by effective articulation. Multiple images by Andy Warhol give rhythm to the steps of people moving across the bridge and mark their progression from one end of the house to the other. Design: Lembo Bohn; Photo: Peter Paige

Modern design respects the true nature of materials, as in this hammered and twisted balustrade that gives appropriate expression to wrought iron. Wooden flooring is jazzed up with cobalt-blue anodyne dye, but the boards and grain still are visible through the transparent color. Design: Brian Murphy Architects; Photo: Tim Street-Porter

Themes of outdoors and indoors are juxtaposed in this entry, where lines and shadows from louvers and mullions seem to bar the outside world and translucent glass flirts with letting it in. Design: Josh Schweitzer, Schweitzer BIM; Photo: Tim Street-Porter

This hall alcove offers considerable storage behind cabinetry designed on a strict grid. The silver wood stain on the cupboard doors complements the metal materials of the table and chairs. Design: Terron Schaeffer; Photo: Tim Street-Porter

Continue unique design elements, such as an inlaid floor pattern, throughout the transition areas of a house for a cohesive effect. Here, doors and interior windows also share a unifying motif, even in the bedroom wing, where transparent glass is replaced with frosted panes for privacy. Design: Jerry Allen Kler and Associates; Photos: John Sutton

Contemporary design celebrates pared-down
expressions of form and function. Striking cantilevered treads, truly a tour de force of
Modernism, distill stairs into their simplest form.
Design: Damga Design; Photo: Peter Paige

Balustrades offer myriad opportunities for creativity. Here, the handrail is an architectural element stepped to look like a stairway itself. Pure white immerses the viewer in the beauty of form in space, with shafts of sunshine moving in an ever-changing pool of light. Design: Wally Cunningham, Architect; Photo: Tim Street-Porter

Glittering in the sun, the meeting point of two glass walls refracts sunlight and projects dramatic diamonds of light on the floor. The result is intense energy at the confluence of the two corridors, one of which leads to the bedroom wing, the other to public spaces. Design: Dirk Denison and Adrian Luchini; Photo: Balthazar Korab

Along a wide corridor, a long table with chairs provides a place for studying or working on art projects. True to contemporary design's emphasis on harmonizing relationships between the interior and exterior, the painted-concrete floor surface is the same throughout the sightline, outside the glass wall as well as in. Design: Frank Lloyd Wright; Photo: Phillip Ennis

In smaller contemporary homes, circulation spaces often serve dual functions. Here, a stair landing provides just enough room for a simple built-in desk and Modern chair.
Design: Fernau and Hartmann Architects; Photo: Tim Street-Porter

Highly polished black slate with an oak border ties together the entrance, halls, and stairways of this contemporary home. A long wooden divider between the living room and stair provides storage and display space without interfering with the open concept of the house or interrupting the flow of light from clerestory windows. Design: David Austin, Austin Patterson Disston Architects; Photos: Fred George

Focus on one or two key pieces of furniture to give entrances a contemporary flavor. Here, two landmark twentieth-century styles are incorporated: a semicircular chair designed by Scottish architect Charles Rennie Mackintosh, and a stylized console inspired by the Art Deco movement. Design: Damga Design; Photo: Peter Paige

Contemporary style revels in personal expression. Remarkable crystal glass doors immediately reveal to all who enter an important part of the homeowner's personality: a passion for dazzling art and fine craftsmanship. Interior Design: Julie Hove; Glass Design: Jerry Cebe, Farallon Studios; Photo: Jim Grove

In this formal entry and stair hall, a post-Modern approach extrapolates from and simplifies classical motifs such as columns, arches, and newel posts with decorative terminals. The overall effect is refined yet lighthearted. Design: Stephen Ackerman, Environetics; Photo: Phillip Ennis

Entrances merit special attention in contemporary homes, as the architectural detailing and furnishings first encountered set the stage for the overall design scheme. A few well-chosen elements—an abstract painting, an avant-garde lamp, a single table by a Modern master—will establish the desired mood. Use color and light to celebrate the form and function of all circulation spaces, including stairways and halls.

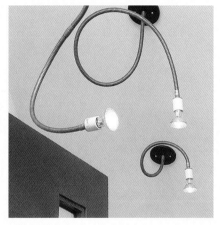

On the Table

Tables in entryways meet pratical needs and provide contemporary style, whether a Modern pedestal-based table, an artistic wrought-iron console, or a trio of inexpensive folding tables.

Making Light

For a welcoming glow and up-to-date attitude, choose from the wide variety of contemporary light fixtures, from pendants to innovative mirror reflector lamps.

Color My World

(**left and above**) Use color to empahsize architectural elements such as stair stringers and support structures. (*above*) Design: Stuart Disston, Austin Patterson Disston Architects; Photo: John Kane

Move It

Use designs and materials in ways that mark and emphasize movement in transition areas, such as regularly placed artwork or framed openings.

Upstairs, Downstairs

Celebrated for their basic form, stairs become sculpture in many contemporary interiors.

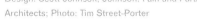

Contemporary
Living Rooms

Contemporary living rooms, despite strong ties to Modernism, break free from the serious, strictly governed design of previous decades.

 The evolution of contemporary style is apparent on paging through the 1952 catalog of Herman Miller, the pioneering Modern furniture manufacturing firm. Then, furniture was placed in stiff arrangements that seem oddly formal and constrained; now, seating is meant to encourage interaction and intimate conversation. Then, sofas were lean with thin, tight cushions that demanded upright posture; now, they invite curling up in deep-cushioned comfort. Then, clear-cut rules of Modern design thinking were followed; now, personal preferences and idiosyncrasies take precedence over abstract principles.

As a result, contemporary living rooms are eclectic in their liberal mixing of furniture and decorative objects from various styles and movements of the twentieth century. A consistent trend, however, is the inclusion of at least one important piece of Modern furniture: for instance, the chaise longue designed by Le Corbusier, Pierre Jeanneret, and Charlotte Perriand in 1928; Eileen Gray's distinctive asymmetrical side table of tubular steel; Charles and Ray Eames's famous 1956 leather and bent plywood lounge chair and ottoman. The list expands as furniture pieces from today's best designers are acclaimed contemporary classics.

This fascination with great furniture extends to an affinity for vibrant contemporary art, another must-have in today's living rooms. Proper display and directed illumination are vital to drawing attention to each work and to creating a considered gallery ambience.

Popular options for living-room floors include solid expanses of wood, slate or stone tiles, waxed concrete, and terrazzo. Furniture often floats uninterrupted on the bare surface. When an expansive living room is open to other areas in the house, however, an area rug adds definition and warmth. Sisal and other textured woven carpet materials are reliable choices.

In response to the current emphasis on comfort, contemporary designers are exploring luxurious upholstery such as velvet, heretofore associated only with opulent traditional interiors. At the other end of the spectrum lie versatile cotton duck, with its casual air, and whimsical renditions of 1940s-vintage patterned fabrics. Leather, of course, is the all-time favorite in contemporary living rooms.

Great Modern furniture has an uncanny ability to adapt to a variety of architectural materials, whether sleekly polished or, as shown, rough-hewn exposed pine beams and stone. Seen here: a round table by Isamu Noguchi, a pair of Mies van der Rohe's Barcelona stools, and two calfskin-covered tubular chairs by Le Corbusier, Le Corbusier and Perriand. Design: Scott Johnson; Johnson, Fain and Partners Architects; Photo: Tim Street-Porter

Art is an important component of contemporary residences. Here, paintings are mounted on an inventive rolling panel system made of industrial metal mesh, enabling the owner to easily change the images on view as the mood strikes.
Design: Drake Design Associates; Photo: Peter Paige

This living room takes an aesthetic cruise through recent decades, pulling together a recently designed avant-garde Italian rolling cart; streamlined seating inspired by mid-century furniture; and the famous chaise longue designed in the late 1920s by Le Corbusier, Jeanneret, and Perriand.
Design: Marc Klein; Photo: Bill Rothschild

Decisive splashes of color invigorate this Spartan environment, as do the gleaming surfaces of the tubular-steel furniture bases and stairway. The sparseness of Modernism means the style can be achieved with a very few well-chosen items.
Photo courtesy of Knoll

The current owner of this early 1960s house, which was designed by pivotal architect Richard Neutra, brings a contemporary sensibility to the interior design. Great pieces of furniture dating from the 1930s through the 1950s are liberally mixed. Included are George Nelson's Coconut chair in gold upholstery, Eero Saarinen's white polyester side table, Charles and Ray Eames's plywood coffee table, and Mies van der Rohe's Barcelona seating.

Design: John Solomon; Photos: Tim Street-Porter

In a dramatic renovation of a 1950s ranch house, a second level was added to create
a massive two-story living room from whose central volume all other spaces flow.
Numerous design elements keep the space from being overwhelming and impersonal:
warm lighting, engaging architectural detailing, large-scale furniture, harmonious
woods and textures, and display areas for the owners' collection of primitive art.
Design: James Edwin Choate, Surber Barber Choate & Hertlein Architects; Photos:
Rion Rizzo, Creative Sources

The dominant architectural element—a massive, curving wall painted cool aqua—builds on Le Corbusier's idea of punched windows in thick walls. In contrast to the architectural openness, the curved white laminated tables and casual sofas form a nest that embraces human connection. Design: Frank Fitzpatrick; Photos: Tim Street-Porter

A basic high-rise apartment is given architectural personality by a simple device: a scored plaster wall that stretches from the living room to an adjacent study. The vintage Modern furniture was purchased at auction and refurbished and reupholstered in graphic, highly textured fabrics. Design: UrbanDesign and Lloy Hack Associates; Photos: Warren Jagger

This vintage Modern house retains the style's affinity for horizontal geometry, from the fireplace bricks whose grout is raked to emphasize horizontal lines to the striped shadows formed by sunlight streaming through venetian blinds. The profusion of throw pillows on the modular sofa is a nod to the contemporary emphasis on comfort. Design: Daniel Sachs; Photo: Tim Street-Porter

A gleaming terrazzo floor, its surface unbroken by rugs, serves as a continuous plane that connects each discrete item of furniture. The au courant design of the sofa and chairs derives from Art Deco's free-form furniture made with tight upholstery techniques. Design: Larry Totah Design; Photo: Tim Street-Porter

The quality of modularity—an important
concept in Modernism—is emphasized
in this airy room. In a post-Modern
twist, the strict grid on the fireplace
wall is broken by the graceful curve
of the mantelpiece. A contemporary
approach also is evident in the slipcov-
ered sofas, whose chaise-style design
speaks to comfort and encourages
lounging. Design: Barbara Barry;
Photos: Tim Street-Porter

A relatively formal aesthetic comes through in this living room, primarily because of an emphasis on balance in the furniture arrangement and display of decorative objects. The overall symmetry, along with a muted palette, makes a serene, quiet space. Design: John Tobeler; Photo: David Duncan Livingston

While neutrals are a perennial favorite in contemporary environments, pale tints of colors strike an unusual note while still providing a restful setting. This harmonious trio of matched upholstered pieces creates a unified design, accented by an ample glass-topped coffee table and bold avant-garde paintings. Photo courtesy of Cassina USA

A palette of neutrals respects this room's dominant architectural features—extensive glazing that dissolves the boundary between inside and out, a linear aesthetic emphasizing horizontal forms, and a remarkable lead screen ledge supported by buttresses along a glass wall. A range of twentieth-century designers is represented in the furniture, from Frank Lloyd Wright to Philippe Starck. Design: David Hertz, Syndesis; Photo: Tim Street-Porter

This bold room spotlights an extensive collection of contemporary art in an enormous space while supporting social interaction. The solution centers on a layout that features two conversation-oriented furniture groupings defined by area rugs. Design: Bershad Design Associates; Photo: Warren Patterson

The designer of this small living room captures contemporary style's wit and confident mixing of furniture and objects. Design: Sean Stussy; Photo: Tim Street-Porter

In this present-day rendering of a room with traditional architecture, most of the seating and tables float in free space rather than rest against a wall, a characteristic typical of contemporary furniture plans. Charles Rennie Mackintosh's sculptural black chair, however, sits like a shy, idiosyncratic guest in the corner, its slender, taut lines accentuated by white walls. Design: Francoise Theise, Adesso; Photo: Eric Roth

The right furniture can transform an older house with a traditional fireplace and moldings into a decidedly contemporary setting. This room's upholstered pieces have simple lines, conveying a restrained elegance that is both up-to-date and adaptable. Design: Kelly Lasser; Photo: David Duncan Livingston

The curved, organic coffee table
and the swirling pattern on the
oversized pillows provide soft-
edged contrast to the rectilinear
expression of the architecture
and the steel windows. Juxtapositions of such seemingly disparate
elements are typical of contemporary style. Design: Josh
Schweitzer, Schweitzer BIM;
Photo: Tim Street-Porter

With tongue in cheek, this living area expresses television as art, with nine sets placed like pictures on the wall. Confident contemporary eclecticism pervades the room, which brings together a flower-power area rug, Isamu Noguchi's luminaires made of China paper, a minimalist coffee table by Charles and Ray Eames, and a vivid color scheme straight out of the 1960s. Design: Stamberg Aferiat Architecture for B&B Italia; Photo: Paul Warchol, courtesy of B&B Italia

The contemporary fascination with unaffected materials is evident in this sprawling living area. The room is dominated by heavy wooden beams and an in-situ concrete load-bearing wall whose exposed pattern and texture express the plywood forms in which the concrete was poured. Design: Mark Mack Architects; Photo: Tim Street-Porter

While the architecture of this house owes much to the residential design of Frank Lloyd Wright, the current owner takes a contemporary approach to furniture, mixing styles, offering ease, and focusing on a tight conversational grouping. Design: Eric Tafel, Architect; Photo: Eric Roth

This high-rise, urban living room designed for nighttime drama uses track lighting and recessed low-voltage lamps to accentuate classic Modern furniture, a lifelike ceramic sculpture by Doug Jeck, and a gleaming, elliptical wooden vessel by Ed Moulthrop. the walls, slate floor, and display pedestal are all black, which de-emphasizes the space itself while allowing the objects in the room to assert the clarity and sensuality of their forms, lines, and textures. Design: Gandy/Peace; Photos: Chris A. Little

While many contemporary interiors take their cue from Modernism's austerity, others are highly luxurious. Plush, richly colored upholstery dominates the aesthetic of this pleasurable room, with finely wrought architectural details and beautiful lighting adding to the sensuous effect.
Design: Mojo Stumer Architects; Photo: Phillip Ennis

A symmetrical seating arrangement increases the formality of this otherwise free-form loft space, while an area rug gives the chairs and sofa a solid sense of place amid the space's volume. A rectilinear screen not only provides privacy while permitting natural light to enter, but also reinforces the sense of structure through its orderly geometry. Design: Machine-Age Corporation; Photo: Eric Roth

In a room lacking a fabulous view or fireplace, create a focal point through a single element whose design makes a strong statement. The floor-to-ceiling media center and storage unit, with its high-contrast coloring and striking linear geometry, has the verve necessary to carry this room. A powerful spotlight caps the composition. Design: Techler Design Group; Photo: Warren Jagger

Living Rooms
details

Today's living rooms emphasize communication. Sofas and chairs are often grouped around a focal point like a fireplace, storage wall, or imposing piece of art—always in a way that enhances conversation. Architectural materials and fabrics span an enormous range; select carefully to bend the ambience toward casual or luxurious while remembering the importance of clearly expressed line and form.

Hot Stuff

The fireplace, giving proper emphasis to the hearth as center of the home, establishes the tone of a living room. In contemporary design, fireplaces range from rough fieldstone to polished slate, from taut Modernist constructions to sensuous sculptural designs.

Line It Up

Consciously incorporate linear architectural detailing—whether horizontal, vertical, or on the diagonal—as a key design element in contemporary living rooms. Photo (*below*) courtesy of Poliform USA

Stylish Upholstery

Up-to-date upholstery options range from the ever-popular leather and ethereal pure white to the latest in luxurious velvets, chenilles, and other high-touch fabrics.

Art Smarts

Beautifully lit contemporary paintings, prints, sculpture, and collections are integral to today's living rooms, which often are reminiscent of sophisticated galleries.

Up Against a Wall

Built-in storage walls and freestanding storage units, important living room pieces during the golden of Modernism, continue to be attractive, functional design elements that help minimize clutter in contemporary homes. Chaise design (*top*): Antonio Citterio and Paolo Navo for B&B Italia: Photo courtesy of B&B Italia

Photo courtesy of Cassina USA

Contemporary
Dining Areas

Dining-room design is not straightforward anymore. Nowadays stock formulas are replaced with solutions

tailored to specific individuals and families. A contemporary approach to design invites people to decide for

themselves what dining should be.

Time was when dining-room design was formulaic. A chandelier, preferably crystal, was centered over a hierarchical rectangular table surrounded by chairs with padded seats and hard backs, with armchairs at the head and foot lording over the side seating. A massive freestanding buffet stood against the wall like a silent, reliable butler.

When designing your contemporary dining area, set aside formulas and consider, first, how formal or informal you intend mealtime to be, how leisurely or high speed. Is the goal to encourage intimacy among dining companions? Or does fostering enjoyment of a stunning skyline view take precedence?

Once such questions are answered, design can manipulate a space to create the desired effect. Simply placing a table on an area rug creates an island that pulls the focus inward, so the dining experience has more to do with conversation than viewgazing. Lighting also has a powerful effect on mood and social interaction.

Luxurious contemporary rooms where dining is a grand event continue to suit those who enjoy high-style entertaining. In some ways these interiors are reminiscent of yesterday's formal dining rooms, albeit with contemporary furniture and forward-thinking architecture. Today, though, dining areas typically are more open to the rest of the house, and the requisite freestanding buffet now is set into its own architectural niche or— even better—replaced by a sleek built-in element.

The most dramatic changes in the design of contemporary dining areas result from major shifts in lifestyle. People tend to live in a hurry. Not only are they less likely than in past eras to have servants to support elegant entertaining, but many prefer a casual, kicked-back atmosphere anyway. Thus the vast majority of meals eaten at home are consumed in an informal dining area, such as a corner with a café-style table and banquette seating. Even that may be too formal for quick snacks, which are best munched on a space-age stool at a high counter adjacent to the kitchen.

This clean-lined separate room, with a traditional rectangular table and seating at the head and foot, is a contemporary take on formal dining. A recessed ceiling with cove lighting emphasizes the table. However, the relationship between interior and exterior is reinforced by abundant windows and flame-cut granite pavers whose lines pull straight through from the inside out.
Design: Richard Meier Architects; Photo: Tim Street-Porter

The angular forms of chairs designed by Philippe Starck mirror the geometry of the ceiling in this nineteenth-century former carriage house. The terra-cotta tones of exposed brick from the original structure influenced selection of the Art Deco-inspired rug and the table with Venetian plaster bases. Interior Design: Lloy Hack Associates; Architecture: Based on a design by William P. Bruder; Photo: Warren Jagger

This dining venue focuses on the terrace view, with a vertically operating door and loose-flowing drapes ready to blow in the wind like cabana draperies. The head of the table is left open without a chair, which both implies less-formal dining and ensures that the view is unin-terrupted. Design: Wanaselja Architecture; Photo: John Sutton

This contemporary design is a poem in glass, turning dining into an ethereal experience. A wall of textured glass blocks contrasts with the table's flat plate glass, while crackle glass is incorporated into the clever suspended fixtures made of long, black flashlights. Design: Brian Murphy Architects; Photo: Tim Street-Porter

Surprising tongue-in-cheek combinations enliven contemporary style. Here, silver-leaf chairs, their formality implying solidity and permanence, are partnered with a wheeled table whose very essence is movement and impermanence. Design: Lembo Bohn; Photo: Peter Paige

This house offers two casual dining options side by side: Spartan benches placed at a picnic-like table and stools drawn up to a kitchen counter. The barstools have an amusing beehive look, suggesting that dining on them is a fleeting, lighthearted activity.
Design: David Hertz, Syndesis; Photo: Tim Street-Porter

Putting it all together is clearly a matter of personal taste in this eclectic room. Traditional architecture and appointments are mixed with a table designed by Le Corbusier and whimsical French garden folding chairs. Design: Veronique Louvet; Photo: Eric Roth

Placing a table in a geometrically eccentric relationship to the walls lends an informal ambience, as do chairs of varying design. This line of seating allows deliberate variation in both the back cut-out design and type of finish of the chairs. Design: Frank Israel; Photo: Tim Street-Porter

Custom tables, through materials and other design elements such as line and form, create a cohesive look by integrating furniture with the architecture. Here, a table of pine and stainless steel harmonizes with the pine floor. Design: Fernau and Hartmann Architects; Photo: Tim Street-Porter

By selecting a few graceful elements, an elegant dining setting can be created even when a house's open floor plan implies casualness. Here, an oval etched-glass table hovers lucidly amid Mario Bellini's leather Cab chairs, which consist of a tight skin of leather zippered over a metal frame. Design: Larry Totah Design; Photo: Tim Street-Porter

In a wonderful expression of contemporary design's witty juxtapositions, three formal crystal chandeliers hang together above a down-home floor of high-gloss painted boards. A raised glass tabletop with a silver bucket of flowers implies polished sophistication, while diners sit on the most basic, utilitarian steel office chairs painted with white enamel. Design: Brian Murphy Architects; Photo: Tim Street-Porter

This dining area retains a strong connection to the kitchen not only by proximity but also by use of the same granite flooring and polished chrome. Laced leather-upholstered chairs by Mies van der Rohe repeat the taut efficiency of the kitchen's design, as does a table by sculptor Isamu Noguchi that seems to float on a web of steel rods. Design: Drake Design Associates; Photo: Peter Peirce

Even in a small residence, on-the-go snacking is accommodated in addition to more leisurely dining at an adjacent
table. A diverse collection of furniture and glassware from
the 1940s and 1950s creates an exuberant, joyful setting.
Photo: Eric Roth

Color unites furniture and architecture into a painterly composition of rectangular forms. The powerful ability of color to establish a strong sense of place, even in a small area, is illustrated in this unusual dining room. Design: Stamberg Aferiat Architecture for B&B Italia; Photo: Paul Warchol, courtesy of B&B Italia

In dining areas with open architecture, chairs with solid backs and plush upholstery can create a sense of enclosure and warmth around the table. The spaciousness of this room is accentuated by a mirrored wall. Design: Interiors by M & S; Photo: Phillip Ennis

Here, the chairs backs are open, but visual weight arising from their dark color and rectilinear form gathers diners inward for intimate dining despite the surrounding circulation space. Design: Stuart Narofsky, Architect; Photo: Phillip Ennis

This space restricts the palette to black, white, and gray out of respect for a significant art collection and the remarkable curved forms of Art Nouveau dining chairs designed by Josef Hoffman. Pendant light fixtures incorporate ball details inspired by the chairs. Design: Stephen Ackerman, Environetics; Photo: Phillip Ennis

In a soaring pavilion-like space, several features work together to make dining a noteworthy occasion: a sisal rug defines a clear boundary; the table has a distinct, solid presence; and stage lights beam powerful rays directly onto the table from high in the exposed rafters.
Custom Table: Fox Brothers Furniture; Photo: Eric Roth

Bright color is the dominant design element in this dining room,
seen in the furniture accents, boldly patterned glazed pottery, and
architectural detailing. The lighthearted mood implies that mealtimes
here are fun and uninhibited. Design: Sharon Campbell Interior
Design; Photo: David Duncan Livingston

A wide range of dining locations and furniture is available to contemporary designers. When a glass-topped table with a garden pedestal base is placed by a wall of windows and French doors opening to a patio, mealtime takes on the flavor of al fresco dining. Photo: David Duncan Livingston

Contemporary contrasts give this dining room unique character. Highly rectilinear architectural elements create a backdrop with a clean, graphic quality that sets off the compound curves of the eccentric upholstered chairs. Design: Mojo Stumer Architects; Photo: Phillip Ennis

Amid a busy circulation space, a plaid floor of blue and white tiles gives this dining area its due. The design is an energetic dance of parallel and perpendicular lines in the floor tiles, stair detailing, window blinds, red chair backs, and channeled banquette cushions. Design: Ken Payson; Photo: Tim Street-Porter

When dining is open to nearby rooms and a serene, peaceful interior design is desired, select aesthetically compatible furniture united through similar textures, woods, and colors. Design: Lloy Hack Associates; Photo: Warren Jagger

This dining area makes mealtime less serious but not less pleasurable. Easy comfort comes from cushioned banquette seating, a table large enough to accommodate serving platters, and a pendant fixture that pools light to focus attention inward. Unexpected guests are welcome, such as the colorful reptile sculpture darting up the wall and chairs that are cousins to tin watering cans. Design: Dan Phipps and Associates; Photo: John Sutton

In an example of the contemporary interest in contrasting geometries and materials to powerful effect, this dining room's storage elements and built-in buffet feature an arresting asymmetrical design and light anagre wood with ebony detailing. Everything is first class here: the intricate lighting system, the gold-framed print by Marc Chagall, and the confident table and chairs designed by Dakota Jackson. Design: Mojo Stumer Architects; Photo: Phillip Ennis

This luxurious, formal room has all the elements of the most sumptuous traditional dining spaces, including a buffet and display shelving, interpreted with clean-lined contemporary sophistication and architectural curves befitting the sensuous tropical setting. Dakota Jackson designed the grand lace-wood table with ebony detailing, surrounded by comfortable upholstered chairs. Low-voltage fixtures set into a skylight provide glamorous nighttime illumination. Design: Francis-Russell Design Decoration; Photo: Peter Peirce

Dining Areas

details

Today's dining areas are less fussy than in the past, with durable, easy-to-clean tables and built-in architectural elements that are sculptural and streamlined. An appreciation for simplicity extends to understated centerpieces and pendant light fixtures. Favorite twentieth-century glassware or pottery often is on view, with the emphasis on the objects themselves rather than on display cabinets or shelving.

Up-To-Date Buffets

Modern buffets frequently are integrated into the architecture and use materials consistent with interior detailing. Carts on castors and lightweight tray tables also provide surfaces for food and drink. Design (*center*): Marmol and Radziner Architects; Photo: Tim Street-Porter

Banquette Banquet

With associations of eating in a fun diner or friendly café, banquette seating is making a comeback. Design (*bottom*): Mark Mack Architects; Photo: Tim Street-Porter

Simple Centerpieces

In keeping with contemporary style's appreciation for pure forms, create centerpieces that highlight the organic shapes and colors of fruits and vegetables.

Shelve It

Yesteryear's china cabinets are replaced by dining-room display options running the gamut from inexpensive wall-mounted shelving to finely crafted niches that blend mellifluously into the interior architecture.

Pendant Pizzazz

Pendant fixtures throw illumination down onto the tabletop, providing functional lighting and giving tables a warm glow that draws people in. Recessed adjustable luminaires are another great solution for spotlighting specific areas.

Slick Tabletops

Many of today's tabletops have low-maintenance surfaces such as stone, doing away with the need for tablecloths. Glass is the most popular surface of all, often incorporated into the table design to allow its discrete expression. Table design (*below*): Paolo Piva for B&B Italia; Photo courtesy of B&B Italia

Contemporary
Kitchens

Today's kitchens take seriously the role good food plays in enhancing human life. No matter how technologically oriented society becomes, people continue to seek out ways to be nurtured in the most basic sense. Thus the contemporary kitchen is a bastion not only of efficiency, but also of nurturing.

Once relegated to a dark, out-of-the-way corner in the back of the house, the kitchen is now part of the center of home, a place of airiness and light. Modern kitchens make a point of being open to other primary living areas, separated only by a counter, sliding translucent door, or floating room divider.

The heightened appreciation of food as source of nurturing influences kitchen design in many respects. Massive range hoods and cooktops have become contemporary equivalents of the huge cooking fireplaces of previous centuries. In fact, appliances of all kinds are made for more heavy duty, with commercial-grade refrigerators and ovens having become de rigueur.

As lifestyles have become more casual and entertaining less affected, kitchen design has evolved to encourage socializing. Cooking no longer is a solo activity, but a group event—hence the popularity of the island, a meeting spot that draws people together for food preparation and conversation. In small kitchens, a work table or butcher block on castors serves the same purpose.

Sleek, durable materials typify contemporary kitchens, with stainless steel ranking as the most popular choice for appliances, cabinetry hardware, and numerous other surfaces. Interestingly, the institutional look of stainless steel often is juxtaposed with materials that are typical of yesteryear's residential kitchens, such as fine woods and non-staining natural stone. Glass and mirrors also are embraced by kitchen designers, who use them to reinforce an open ambience.

Kitchens can be the most exciting room in the home for architects and interior designers, who make the most of kitchens' many functional elements either by transforming them into artistic creations or by stripping them down to absolute basics. Everything is fair game for the imagination—a bank of shelves expressed as a cubist structure, a snack bar reminiscent of a flying saucer, or fittings and fixtures that resemble sculpture more than plumbing.

In smaller kitchens where a stationary island might limit flexibility, a mobile table is handy for dining or working. Stainless steel, used in the table, appliances, and cabinetry hardware, is an important accent material in this room. Particularly noteworthy: the cooktop hood, whose pleated form expresses how thin sheets of stainless steel become stronger when folded.
Photo: Tim Street-Porter

This attractive space features many elements found in well-designed contemporary kitchens: a central island that encourages socializing, a stainless-steel cooktop with a sculptural hood, a multilayered lighting system for specific tasks and overall illumination, and an innovative use of exotic wood and natural stone. Design: Dan Phipps and Associates; Photo: John Sutton

A simple arched plane made of ash runs between this kitchen and the adjacent dining room, lending contemporary character through its unique, asymmetrical design. In the kitchen, open shelving provides easy access to pots and pans above the range and Vermont marble countertops. Design: McKee Patterson, Austin Patterson Disston Architects; Photos: John Kane

Kitchen renovations often extend into areas where existing windows are lower than standard counter height. A table-level dining counter and bank of low cabinets solve the problem while affording maximum enjoyment of outdoor views. Design: Sean Stussy; Photo: Tim Street-Porter

Exquisite wood surfaces and stone tiles give this compact open kitchen a sophisticated look that blends well with adjacent living areas. The cabinetry and walls are akin to finely crafted furniture. Design: Stedila Design; Photo: Richard Mandelkorn

To make kitchens user-friendly, install several sources of indirect lighting rather than a single fixture that blasts light throughout the room. Here, uplighting from sconces rakes off the canted ceiling to provide an indirect ambient glow. This space also receives natural light from the fabulous ocean view in the adjacent room; daylight filters through the kitchen's translucent sliding door, open or closed. Design: Shubin + Donaldson Architects; Photo: Farshid Assassi

Etched glass panels used in cabinets and the central island incorporate openness, a popular theme in contemporary design. Glass lightens the visual weight of the cabinetry and allows natural light from exterior glass doors to penetrate the room, even below counter level.
Design: Brian Murphy Architects;
Photo: Tim Street-Porter

Texture is an important contemporary design element, even in kitchens. This room features an impressive range of textures: cabinetry with a mirror-like polyester finish; door insets of ribbed glass; and a shiny stainless-steel backsplash with a geometric grid pattern.
Photo courtesy of Wood-Mode

A playful approach to color accents, seen here in cabinetry and dishes, establishes a buoyant atmosphere in kitchens large and small. Sunshine streaming in from a skylight adds to the upbeat ambieance, illuminating the island and book-lined balcony. Design: Marmol and Radziner Architects; Photos: Tim Street-Porter

Strong colors can be used in compact areas, as long as they are edited to one or two tones. This kitchen's lively, saturated blue carries through to the tiles, countertops, woodwork, and sink. Extending the cool-colored tiles on the wall surfaces results in a strong, consistent foil for the warm, rich wood of the cabinets. Design: John A. Buscarello; Photo courtesy of Wood-Mode

Color can be a powerful ally when creating a contemporary kitchen that stands out from the norm. A wall of
bright red adds personality to this white kitchen, where
the island cooktop's pendulum-style hood doubles as a
shelf for ingredients and pans. Photo courtesy of
Becker Zeyko

Contemporary residential kitchens often incorporate ideas and equipment from their commercial counterparts, an approach that drives this design. A skylight illuminates the center of the room, which is dominated by a massive square surface, half reserved for food preparation and the other composed of two mobile tables. The unexpected fur upholstery of the secretarial chairs adds a witty comment. Design: Brian Murphy Architects; Photo: Tim Street-Porter

Using a single material—here, stainless steel—on the surfaces of the cabinets, countertops, refrigerator, stove, sink, and trash compactor keeps a small kitchen from seeming chopped up and dominated by appliances. Design: Antoine Kripacz; Photo: Tim Street-Porter

In this ingenious galley kitchen, a green tile surface becomes a strong graphic element as it drops from the backsplash, down the wall, and onto the floor. A tiny window peeks out beneath the secondary sink, whose chrome-plated plumbing fittings have the status of decorative objects. Photos: Tim Street-Porter

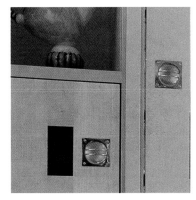

This room is a wonderful marriage of contemporary elements, such as the cabinetry's detailing and hardware, and more traditional features, such as a drop-in porcelain sink and classic stone tile floor. Because its materials and forms are so elegant, the kitchen need not make any apologies for its openness to the formal dining room beyond. Design: Olson Lewis & Dioli Architects; Photo: Eric Roth

A dramatic example of the openness of contemporary kitchen design, this room soars to the second story, where a bridge allows conversation from one floor to the next as cooking aromas waft upward. Photo courtesy of Becker Zeyko

A portion of the cabinet juts out to provide an angled surface that promotes working and socializing in the absence of a communal island. Daylight enters through an exterior wall of glass blocks. Photo courtesy of Becker Zeyko

This kitchen showcases the range of storage options available in contemporary design: open shelving, cabinets with solid doors, and a grid of cabinets with textured glass fronts. Photo courtesy of Becker Zeyko

Striking black-tile flooring and black-lacquer counters and backsplashes animate the work area of this contemporary kitchen. Stools with slender stainless-steel bases encourage family and guests to gather during meal preparation. Photo courtesy of SieMatic

While contemporary kitchens typically limit clutter for a cleaner look, utensils, pots, pans, and collectibles are welcome in the open when displayed in a neat, organized way. In this pleasant room, a delightful collection of cups and saucers is presented in a built-in version of an up-to-date shadow box. Design: Foster Associates; Photo: Eric Roth

Most contemporary kitchens are well integrated with the rest of the house. Here, a graceful, curving wooden divider floats to the left of the food-preparation island, with circulation and living space on the other side and a casual dining area at the far end. Design: Pasanella + Klein, Stoltzman + Berg; Photo: Paul Warchol

Glazed ceramic tiles and a banquette eating area evoke the 1950s, while a long skylight and stainless-steel appliances and hardware keep the kitchen nicely up to date. This design illustrates the wisdom of using a few materials well—in this case, dark wood, green tiles, and stainless steel. Design: J. Staff Architect; Photo: Art Gray

Piece by Piece

Kitchens
details

Today's kitchens are out in the open, encouraging people to help prepare food or to socialize around magnets such as a central island, a snack bar, and casual seating. Durable yet beautiful materials—natural stone, exotic woods, surfaces inspired by commercial kitchens—are essential for a contemporary appearance. The look is completed with sleek storage systems, serious appliances, and multilayered lighting with cutting-edge fixtures.

Materials World

Materials give kitchens modern-day flavor, from mirrors for backsplashes, to metals used for everything from tiles to countertops.

Cool Runnings

Choose faucets and fixtures with streamlined styling and special features such as pull-out spray heads and hot-water spouts.

Photo courtesy of Ann Sacks Tile & Stone

Industrial Strength

Heavy-duty stoves, refrigerators, and other appliances once reserved for commercial purposes now give residential kitchens a distinct contemporary edge.

Design: American Classic Kitchens; Photo courtesy of Wood-Mode

Photo courtesy of Kohler Co.

On a Roll

Carts and tables on castors provide the flexibility needed for today's multifunctional kitchens.

Photo below courtesy of Becker Zeyko

Storage Options

While pure **Modernists** keep kitchenware out of sight in appliance garages or behind opaque cabinets, more easygoing contemporary options include cleverly designed pot racks, translucent cabinet doors, and clean-lined open shelving—as long as the result looks well organized.

Photos above courtesy of SieMatic

Hood Ornaments

Cooktop hoods, the contemporary equivalent of yesteryear's massive cooking hearths and chimneys, are now major design elements often rendered in artistic ways.

Design (*top*): Scott Johnson; Johnson, Fain and Partners Architects; Photo: Tim Street-Porter
Photo above courtesy of Becker Zeyko

Contemporary
Bedrooms

In most contemporary bedrooms, style falls midway between minimalism and luxury. While excess is gone in terms of quantity of acquired objects, the quality of elements such as architectural materials, seating, and bed linens is higher than ever. In today's bedrooms, quality definitely reigns over quantity.

For centuries, bedrooms revealed much about money and power. Some kings and queens of yore actually held court in their bedrooms, where the bedstead was as elaborate as a throne, the bed curtains as plush as his majesty's cape.

Until Modernism began revolutionizing design, the royal ideal made its way into the bedroom of anyone who could afford even a modest semblance of it. But the twentieth-century vision reveres restraint rather than opulent abundance, resulting in an effort to do away with the traditional, overwrought bedroom.

To begin, designers in recent decades changed the profile of beds, making them low and lean in contrast with the prevailing wisdom that higher meant softer and better. Placed on humble platforms first introduced by the Scandinavians, everyday beds began to look more like furniture

from a monastery than from a castle. Rather than epitomizing solidity, beds grew lighter, sometimes appearing to hover above the floor.

Today, designers continue to work toward redefining the bedroom. No longer, for instance, is it mandatory to position the head of a bed against a wall. Headboards, while still popular, are selected or rejected according to personal preference. Virtual headboards and canopies playfully reference the real thing; interior architecture and lighting techniques emphasize the head of the bed or create a sense of enclosure.

With characteristic thoughtfulness, contemporary designers consider the quality of the experience of falling asleep and waking in a given environment. More than ever, bedrooms with pleasing outdoor views maximize the exterior connection by featuring extensive windows with translucent drapes, shades, or other treatments that offer privacy but still admit light come morning. Skylights also are extremely popular in today's bedrooms.

A compressed glass ceiling ensures the owners are in touch with nature, whether relaxing in bed or in the Jacuzzi behind the headboard wall. Contrasting with the room's hard-edged steel structure and challenging angles, a sheared fur spread is the ultimate accouterment for luxuriating in bed. Design: Augustin Hernandez; Photo: Tim Street-Porter

Contemporary architecture, with expansive plate-glass windows, typically brings the outside in. Here, though, a bright yellow barn-style door creates an opening large enough to wheel the mobile bed onto a sleeping porch for sweet dreams under the stars. A massive post, with its bark intact, stands au naturel next to nearby tree trunks.
Design: Fernau and Hartmann Architects; Photo: Tim Street-Porter

A combination headboard and room divider made of beautiful anagre wood separates the bed from the adjacent bath area. For a seamless aesthetic, the same granite is used to detail cabinetwork in both parts of the suite. Design: Brayton Hughes Design Studio; Photo: David Duncan Livingston

This bedroom is all about honestly expressed, simply detailed materials. The exposed-steel structure, plywood ceiling, polished concrete floor, and planar wall of etched glass all have Modern flair, making the crystal chandelier over the bed a surprising and witty addition. Design: Brian Murphy Architects; Photo: Tim Street-Porter

Designed as much for self-reflection and avant-garde artistry as for a good
night's sleep, this fantastic bed is suspended from the ceiling by wires. In
an innovative pun on suspended animation, an overhead video camera and
monitor allow for instant play back of the sleeper's every move. Design:
Jane Victor and Jennifer Ellenberg, Jane Victor Associates; Photos:
Norman McGrath, courtesy of American Hospital of Paris French
Designers Showhouse

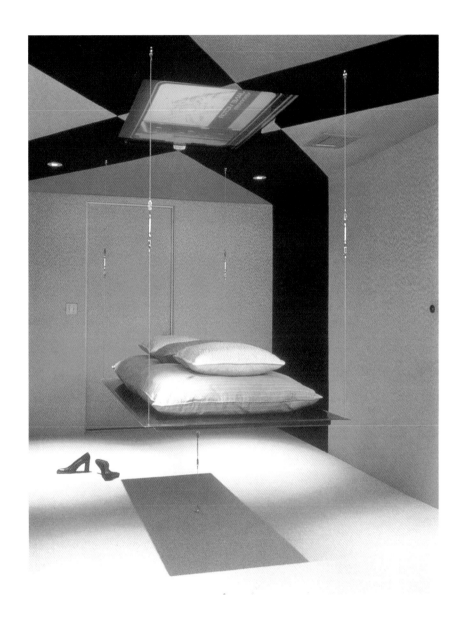

This bedroom's design celebrates light and lightness. Natural light filters in through a diaphanous window treatment, with recessed fixtures illuminating specific areas of the room. The theme plays out in the design of the bed, built-in cabinetry, and window casings, which all give the impression of floating above the floor. Design: Peter L. Gluck and Partners, Architects; Photo: Paul Warchol

A confident sense of style comes through in this modest yet memorable room. Alvar Aalto's Modern lounge chairs are a graceful, restrained element amid a room enlivened by a bright appliqué quilt and stylized lamps that express the jazzier side of 1940s design. Design: Sean Stussy; Photo: Tim Street-Porter

In an unaffected, highly personal expression, this basic bedroom exudes humility in its American checked bedspread and the witty anecdote simply presented above the bed. Design: Daniel Sachs; Photo: Tim Street-Porter

Sometimes a single strong design element elevates a
room beyond the ordinary. Here, an undulating, peach-
colored wall of waxed plaster turns an ordinary bedroom into a space of architectural distinction. Design:
Gary Wolf Architects; Photo: Eric Roth

While many Modern bedrooms minimize or eliminate headboards, this room makes a powerful head-of-the-bed statement despite the modest size of the space. A mirrored closet door doubles the room's perceived size, and the tightly organized palette and unadorned furniture keep the design under control. Design: Terron Schaeffer; Photo: Tim Street-Porter

The bed's orthogonal relationship to the window walls makes it possible to gaze at the garden while lingering in bed. A deep-cushioned perimeter-seating unit invites reading in the sunshine. Design: Frank Gehry; Photo: Tim Street-Porter

Headboards aren't the only way to give emphasis to beds. This sophisticated architectural solution consists of stepped and curved lacquered panels, with downlighting from recessed fixtures casting shadows that reinforce the horizontal geometry. Design: Vince Lattuca; Photo: Phillip Ennis

The simple uplights placed on the floor illuminate the walls and ceiling, giving the light inside this bedroom a drama all its own. In addition, the glittering nighttime cityscape is showcased in an exciting tableau. Design: Saunders & Walsh; Photo: Phillip Ennis

Storage and display of books and objects are accommodated in a head-board wall that includes recessed glass shelving and an alcove for art as well as the bed. Repeated use of a particular fabric—on the chair, bed-skirt, and pillows—has a unifying effect. Design: Stedila Design; Photo: Richard Mandelkorn

It's sleep-a-go-go in this refreshing room where the bed—usually the most luxurious item in the bedroom—makes a minimalist statement somewhere between a go-cart and a hospital gurney. Despite the bed's openness and vulnerability, the curved Venetian plaster wall provides a nurturing sense of enclosure in the gallerylike room.
Design: Piers Gough, CZWG Architects; Photo: Tim Street-Porter

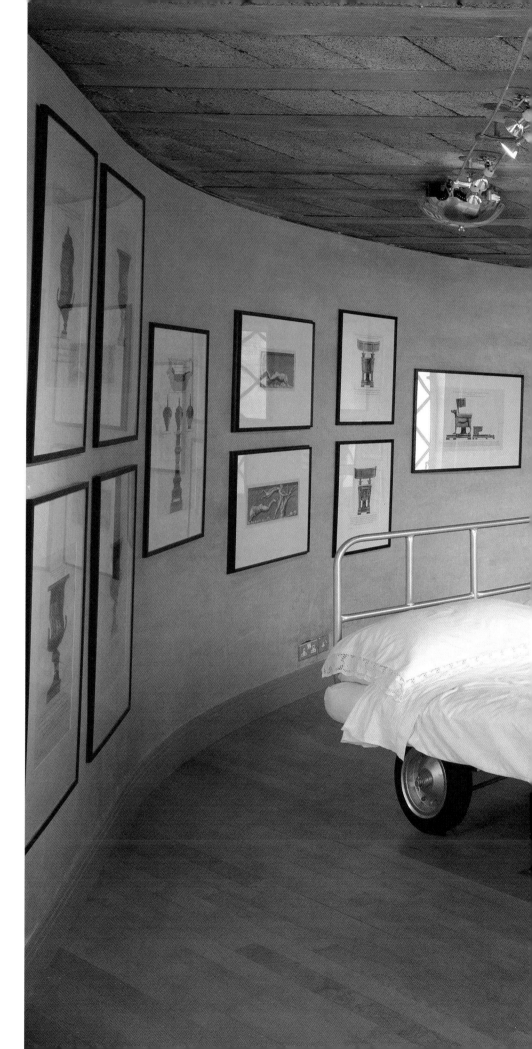

With its focus turned inward rather than out, this bedroom
creates a gray, soft-touch world that is soothing and elegant.
The recessed built-in headboard incorporates a linear incandes-
cent fixture that accentuates the textured fabric walls. Design:
Techler Design Group; Photo: Warren Jagger

Here again the room's focus is inward, but instead of fabric, the primary materials are beautiful pearwood and lacewood, which cover the walls and ceiling like the lining of an exquisite box. This is contemporary custom cabinetwork at its best, with finely detailed diamond insets and refined pulls of brushed stainless steel. Interior Design: Celeste Cooper; Architecture: Adolfo Perez, Architect; Photo: Warren Jagger

Dark, sexy, and compact, this room relies on an eight-foot-square mirror for visual depth. The bed, covered with wool flannel, floats in the middle of the room. Pillows are stored in a closet during the day, which supports the designer's desire to eliminate extraneous items. Beautiful forms are emphasized, with ceramic pots by Claude Conover and Ted Saupe highlighted on pedestals. Design: Gandy/Peace; Photo: Chris A. Little

The contemporary interest in contrasts fuels the design of this room, where large black-and-white panels in a highly structured checkerboard give presence to the head of the bed. The rigid geometry gives way to a flowing, organic aesthetic in the loose, unstructured draperies and the curvilinear forms of the desk, which references the style of Louis XV. Design: Cynthia, Inc.; Photo: Phillip Ennis

Amid fabulous International-style architecture featuring cool, ribbed-glass blocks and an exposed-steel structure, this bedroom offers warm woods and plush linens. The lower part of the glass doors is etched, affording some privacy without excluding the idyllic beach-front view. Design: Barbara Barry; Photo: Tim Street-Porter

This Asian twist on the traditional four-poster bed has the visual cachet necessary to carry the design of the entire room. The open, rectilinear styling of the bed is intriguing when seen from behind and doesn't interfere with the water views seen through a bank of compatible windows. Photo: Paul Rocheleau, courtesy of Thos. Moser Cabinetmakers

Against a Modern architectural aesthetic in which the room's structure is expressed, the contemporary interior design focuses on quiet ease. The bed comforter and the cushions on the built-in seating are soft and inviting, and Mecho shades mute the sunshine while allowing some transparency. Design: Lenny Steinberg; Photo: Tim Street-Porter

While some contemporary bedrooms use architecture to reinterpret the canopy bed, this room uses a simple rectangle of fabric-backed raffia draped over suspended brass rods. The effect is tailored, clean, contemporary. Across the room from the foot of the bed, an Eero Saarinen chair introduces an important design from the Art Deco movement.

Design: Ida Goldstein, Interior Design Applications; Photo: Eric Roth

The bedroom is treated as a unit, with dressing table, storage, writing desk, and night tables all built in for a cohesive aesthetic. Panels of stretched raw silk washed with downlighting accentuate the head of the bed, as do silver and gold lamé shams. The Art Deco-style sham fabric carries through to the chair upholstery. Design: Mojo Stumer Architects; Photo: Phillip Ennis

The intense mustard-green of the walls and ribbed carpet sets this room apart from most contemporary bedrooms, which tend to be neutral. The custom bed of burnished steel and brass adds to the drama, as do the attached mobile night table and integrated lamp. A mirror leaning against the wall yields a larger sense of space. Design: Stedila Design; Photo: Alec Hemer

Piece by Piece *Bedrooms details*

Contemporary design eschews traditional expectations, and today's bedrooms are no exception. The bed can be with or without a headboard, and any spot in the room is fair game for its placement. Keep decorative objects to a few special highlights, and make sure even the most functional items—seating, lamps, tables—have artful flair.

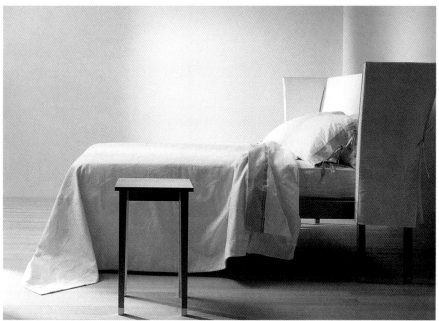

Photo above courtesy of Cassina USA

Floating to Sleep

In times past, beds always were placed against a wall, but today's free-form apprach to design offers the options of floating a bed in the middle of the room. Photo above courtesy of Poliform USA

Head of the Bed

In today's bedrooms, headboards range from complete absence, to upholstered options that are comfortable for reading, to architectural solutions emphasizing the head of the bed through built-in features.

Turning the Tables

Think creatively about bedside tables, which can be sculptural gems echoing materials and forms used elsewhere in the room. Some minimalist modern-day interiors completely eliminate the need for a freestanding table by featuring built-in shelving and wall-mounted lighting or by incorporating a bed whose design includes trays.

Lounging Around

Because bedrooms aren't just for sleeping, provide seating on chairs and chaises lounges that coordinate with the design's overall palette and patterns. Built-in sofas guarantee an indivisible fit with the architecture. Design (*below left*): Frank Israel; Photo: Tim Street-Porter

Photo above courtesy of Cassina USA

Designers and Manufacturers

Francoise Theise
Adesso
200 Boylston Street
Boston, MA 02116

American Classic Kitchens, Inc.
150 East 58th Street
New York, NY 10155

Ann Sacks Tile & Stone
8120 Northeast 33rd Drive
Portland, OR 97211

Austin Patterson Disston Architects
376 Pequot Avenue
P.O. Box 61
Southport, CT 06490

B&B Italia USA
Architects and Designers Building
150 East 58th Street
New York, NY 10155

Barbara Barry
9526 Pico Boulevard
Los Angeles, CA 90035

Becker Zeyko
U.S. Headquarters
1030 Marina Village Parkway
Alameda, CA 94501

Jill Benedict and Peter Stempel
117 Lexington Road
Lincoln, MA 01773

Bershad Design Associates
P.O. Box 15696
Boston, MA 02215

Brian Murphy Architects
147 West Channel Road
Santa Monica, CA 90402

Brayton Hughes Design Studio
250 Sutton
San Francisco, CA 94107

William P. Bruder, Architect
1314 West Circle Mountain Road
New River, AZ 85027

John A. Buscarello
33 Gold Street
New York, NY 10038

Cassina USA
200 McKay Road
Huntington Station, NY 11746

Celeste Cooper
c/o Repertoire, Inc.
300 Boylston Street
Boston, MA 02116

Wally Cunningham, Architect
1102 West Arbor Drive
San Diego, CA 92103

Currimbhoy Design
833 Broadway, Third Floor
New York, NY 10003

Cynthia, Inc.
GSB Building, Suite 711
1 Belmont Avenue
Bala Cynwyd, PA 19004

Piers Gough
CZWG Architects
17 Bowling Green Lane
London ECIR OBD, UK

Damga Design
207 East 76th Street, #2D
New York, NY 10021

Dan Phipps and Associates
131 Post Street
San Francisco, CA 94109

Dirk Denison
754 North Milwaukee Avenue
Chicago, IL 60622

Drake Design Associates, Inc.
140 East 56th Street
New York, NY 10022

Stephen Ackerman
Environetics
116 East 27th Street
New York, NY 10016

Jerry Cebe
Farallon Studios
83 Hamilton Drive, Suite 100
Novato, CA 94949

Fernau and Hartmann Architects
2512 Ninth Street
Berkeley, CA 94710

Frank Fitzpatrick
1637 Silver Lake Boulevard
Los Angeles, CA 90039

Michele Foster
Foster Associates
111 Glen Road
Portsmouth, RI 02871

Fox Brothers Furniture
39 Liberty Street
Newburyport, MA 01950

Billy Francis and Ed Russell
Francis-Russell Design Decoration Inc.
800 Fifth Avenue, Suite 11D
New York, NY 10021

Gandy/Peace Inc.
349 Peachtree Hills Avenue, Suite C2
Atlanta, GA 30305

Gary Wolf Architects Inc.
145 Hanover Street
Boston, MA 02108

Frank Gehry
1520 Cloverfield Boulevard
Santa Monica, CA 90404

Augustin Hernandez
Bosques Ve Acasias 61
Mexico City, Mexico 11700

Julie Hove
2222 Shelter Bay
Mill Valley, CA 94941

Interiors by M & S
14 Clover Lane
Roslyn Heights, NY 11577

Frank Israel
254 South Robertson
Los Angeles, CA 90211

J. Staff Architect
2148-C Federal Avenue
Los Angeles, CA 90025

Jane Victor and Jennifer Ellenberg
Jane Victor Associates
34 West Ninth Street
New York, NY 10011

Jerry Allen Kler and Associates
1306 Bridgeway
Sausalito, CA 94965

Scott Johnson
Johnson, Fain and Partners Architects
800 Wilshire Boulevard, 2nd Floor
Los Angeles, CA 90017

Marc Klein
30 Sycamore Lane
Roslyn Heights, NY 11577

Mary Knackstedt
2901 North Front Street
Harrisburg, PA 17110

Knoll
1235 Water Street
East Greenville, PA 18041

Kohler Co.
444 Highland Drive
Kohler, WI 53044

Larry Totah Design
2912 Colorado Avenue
Santa Monica, CA 90404

Kelly Lasser
2955 Clay Street, #2
San Francisco, CA 94115

Vince Lattuca
c/o Visconti & Co.
245 East 57th Street
New York, NY 10021

Lembo Bohn
1 Gansevoort Street
New York, NY 10014

Lloy Hack Associates Inc.
425 Boylston Street
Boston, MA 02116

Veronique Louvet
140 Campbell Street
Roxbury, MA 02119

Machine-Age Corporation
354 Congress Street
Boston, MA 02210

Mark Mack Architects
246 First Street
San Francisco, CA 94103

Marmol and Radziner Architects
1631 21st Street
Santa Monica, CA 90404

Mojo Stumer Architects
55 Bryant Avenue
Roslyn, NY 11576

Stuart Narofsky, Architect
112 Huntington Road
Port Washington, NY 11050

Olson Lewis & Dioli Architects
17 Elm Street
Manchester-by-the-Sea, MA 01944

Pasanella + Klein, Stoltzman + Berg
330 West 42nd Street
New York, NY 10036

Adolfo Perez, Architect
72 Langley Road
Newton, MA 02159

Peter L. Gluck and Partners, Architects
19 Union Square West, 12th Floor
New York, NY 10003

Poliform USA, Inc.
Architects and Designers Building
150 East 58th Street
New York, NY 10155

Rick Garofalo
Repertoire, Inc.
300 Boylston Street
Boston, MA 02116

Richard Meier Architects
475 Tenth Avenue
New York, NY 10018

Daniel Sachs
10 Greene Street
New York, NY 10013

Saunders & Walsh, Inc.
1438 Third Avenue, #18E
New York, NY 10028

Josh Schweitzer
Schweitzer BIM
5541 West Washington Boulevard
Los Angeles, CA 90016

Sharon Campbell Interior Design
217 Crescent Road
San Anselmo, CA 94960

Shubin + Donaldson Architects
629 State Street, #242
Santa Barbara, CA 93101

SieMatic Corp.
2 Greenwood Square
3331 Street Road, Suite 450
Bensalem, PA 19020

Stamberg Aferiat Architecture
126 Fifth Avenue
New York, NY 10011

Stedila Design
135 East 55th Street
New York, NY 10022

Lenny Steinberg
2517 Ocean Front Walk
Venice, CA 90291

James Edwin Choate
Surber Barber Choate & Hertlein
Architects
1389 Peachtree Street NE
Atlanta, GA 30309

David Hertz
Syndesis
2908 Colorado Avenue
Santa Monica, CA 90404

Edgar Tafel, Architect
14 East 11th Street
New York, NY 10003

Timothy Techler
Techler Design Group, Inc.
46 Waltham Street, Suite 301
Boston, MA 02118

Thos. Moser Cabinetmakers
72 Wright's Landing
P.O. Box 1237
Auburn, ME 04211

John Tobeler
350 Townsend Street, Suite 308
San Francisco, CA 94107

Gloria Urban
UrbanDesign
1200 Western Avenue
Seattle, WA 98101

Karl Wanaselja
Wanaselja Architecture
2792 Shasta Road
Berkeley, CA 94708

Wood-Mode, Inc.
1 Second Street
Kreamer, PA 17833

Photographers

Farshid Assassi
P.O. Box 3651
Santa Barbara, CA 93130

Phillip Ennis
114 Millertown Road
Bedford, NY 10506

Art Gray
171 Pier Avenue, #272
Santa Monica, CA 90405

Jim Grove
1 Mono Lane
San Anselmo, CA 94960

Alec Hemer
81 Bedford Street, #5E
New York, NY 10014

Warren Jagger
150 Chestnut Street
Providence, RI 02903

John Kane
P.O. Box 731
New Milford, CT 06776

Balthazar Korab
P.O. Box 895
Troy, MI 48099

Chris A. Little
P.O. Box 467221
Atlanta, GA 30346

David Duncan Livingston
1036 Erica Road
Mill Valley, CA 94941
www.davidduncanlivingston.com

Richard Mandelkorn
65 Beaver Pond Road
Lincoln, MA 01773

Norman McGrath
164 West 79th Street
New York, NY 10024

Peter Paige
269 Parkside Road
Harrington Park, NJ 07640

Warren Patterson
P.O. Box 620353
Newton Lower Falls, MA 02162

Peter Peirce
307 East 44th Street
New York, NY 10017

Rion Rizzo
Creative Sources Photography
6095 Lake Forrest Drive, #100
Atlanta, GA 30328

Paul Rocheleau
482 Canaan Road
Richmond, MA 01254

Eric Roth
337 Summer Street
Boston, MA 02210

Bill Rothschild
19 Judith Lane
Wesley Hills, NY 10952

Tim Street-Porter
2074 Watsonia Terrace
Los Angeles, CA 90068

John Sutton
8 Main Street
Point San Quentin, CA 94964

Paul Warchol
133 Mulberry Street, #65
New York, NY 10013

Carol Meredith writes about interior design and architecture for magazines, newspapers, and professional design firms. During her fifteen years in the field, she has served as managing editor for *Texas Homes* magazine, and home and garden editor for *New England Living*. Her articles have also appeared in *Design Times, Boston* magazine, and the *Boston Globe*. She is author of the recent books, *Eclectic Style in Interior Design* and *Room by Room: Country Interiors*. Ms. Meredith lives in New Hampshire with her husband, David Reynolds, and step-daughters Anne and Aleisha.